CROWN of EGGSHELL

Rachel Deering

ISBN: 9798605698456

Published by Cerasus Poetry
London N22 6LY

www.cerasuspoetry.com

For Gina

because everyone needs at least one human
who loves the whole of you,
darkness and all,
with their whole heart.

Contents

III

Questions That Are Clenched Fists, But The Answers Are Just Stones

IV

In This Story, The Heroine Dies, Then Learns To Live Again

I

In The Myth Of Me,
I Am Geese In Flight

A Return

I carried poetry back in my pocket,
or sometimes it was heavier baggage,
at other times, a gun:
words for parting shots,
words for war.
I returned, a black egg nested
under one arm.
Some say I am part bear, part human,
or perhaps that I had killed bears
for sport, who can remember?
I left so long ago
and this is the way legends grow:
words weave stronger,
truths foggier,
with each mouth that forms to tell them,
to feed the needs of the speakers
who breathe
the air of these tales.

I had killed men,
that much was true.
Murder haunted the hollows
beneath my eyes.
I came back more animal,
more brute.
I returned, as though I had risen
clay-footed from the mud.
Old women sucked their teeth
at the sight of me;
those witches saw deep into the stain of glut of blood –
saw that I had fought for nothing,
the nothing that those who have battled
find they've fought for in the end -
and then recoiled with the disgust
that curdled in the folds of their minds.

The older men craved me,
took lecherous note that my thighs,
a gateway to what had once been firmly closed,
were now left off the latch
and imagined themselves between them,
yet I would not let these patriarchs back in.

I winched up my groaning dawns
and existed in isolation,
as I, in death-bloat,
could no longer stomach the living,
or that I had become something less than solid.
I found irony too – all the undiscovered magic
of my potential innocence,
to which I had hitched such hope when I departed - and now,
womanhood restored, though some men brimmed and brewed
with feigned enchantment for me,
I saw that these were little more than card tricks,
a conceit that I bore this burden of poetry,
not as a bear, but a donkey for the soul.

The Post-Trauma Of Jupiter

Revolve me,
beside Europa or Ganymede,
compliant with and corrupted by
my gravitational pull.
My hurricane atmospheres,
across vacant skies
and corrosive cumulations,
belie that I am nothing,
nothing solid, at least,
at core.
And my violent existence:
bloody,
metallic,
traumatic;
these experiences forged me,
until I became too distant to reach.
I writhe and turn here,
in grip of red spot,
unhealed, an agony
of my solar plexus.
This burn of isolation
is the homelessness
of the landless.
I orbit in toxic shame,
on the outskirts of this solar system.
I rotate in my gigantic pain,
encircled by many wordless moons.

Naked

You have seen this nakedness
and how the skin bruises.
Its cast of Mercury leads the dance
of the rise and fall of craters,
its transit plays the music of my slow death.
You have seen this black egged chick,
that roosts now beneath an arm.
A cuckoo myself,
I could not turn her out –
my feathered orphan.
Do you see the vacancy of nurture
in the way my body bends and
gathers in its yearn for comfort?
And my own inner child, who weeps, inconsolable,
that I carry clutched to hip?
I act, move, respond, speak,
with all the lessons I was taught
and deeper in, my heart waits
between wing beats
for the peck of a promise,
of the love it has sought.

An Agriculture Of Souls

Whilst the cow lows in the field,
hooves in her own shit,
you can hear her approach
in knell of bell from neck.
She warns she is cud-drunk
on lush grass
and bullish in the dark.

The farmer polishes his fists,
drinks his own poison.
He thinks he wrestles his own unseen ghosts,
yet it is he who frightens all the little living things.
He nips and clips their childish wings,
spews his sour breath secrets,
rewrites their histories and
teaches his lessons in metal.

These seedlings, plucked
in their first show of green,
this agriculture of beings
as, beneath the black hollows of stars put out,
he snips the delicate leaves
from their shoots and branches.

No Succour For The Dead

There is no succour for the dead,
though they may have more need of it
than the living.
I have been dead for a number of years now –
perhaps seven, maybe eight.
Some say it was the love that did me in,
but I think it could have been the hate.

And I see how the river
shivers, in certain lights, to grey.
It sings its own harmony
and bears this flotsam of me
to eddy and sink,
out of tune with the encounter.
Hard to resist this tug, the hoodwink
of watery nurse, to slip away.
They pull you out, of course,
pump you and prick you, zombie.
They bring you round again,
stitch you up again, zombie.
Dead and alive again,
they revive you as revenge
for more inventive cycles
of suffering, under a sky blinkered
by clouds, that resolves
to reform for another day.

And before all this, was there something before?
There must have been some history
that preceded this stranglehold of thought,
when I was caught in this barbed snare.
My malaise lifts and lightens in early spring,
in the first flash of orange beak of blackbird,
but then it sifts my head for darkness, once more.
No succour comes.
There is no succour for the dead.

Survival

Our Sun flames the tops of leafless aspens
and in the absence of a breeze, it scalds
even the stones.
This overworked ground
pulses and waits,
ruptures in the dryness,
under a sky emptied of its clouds
and air that has lost its songs.

Here, I cannot see any reflection
of burnt, dust-dirt face.
I am Martian. I am fixed.
Even my tears are salt-baked;
they escape through faults of circumstance
and time and place and
unintended loss of will.

I shall crouch in these vestiges of shade,
with my viper, who cheats
me out of words; as life retreats,
no succour comes. I grasp for
those last seeds of survival,
before all incentive for action drains away,
for there will be no revival,
until it rains one day.

A Return To The Sea

At first, the soft fleshiness
of my humanity
rebelled
against the jar of foam
and spray
in the unevenness of this ocean, as it ambushed
and retreated from
the shore. The threat of gull screamed
overhead –
naked of pretension,
my skin pricked porous,
raw in chill,
febrile.
Limbs persisted,
further in, further in,
mind pulsed and waited,
lungs hesitated in caution, but yielded
to the sea.
Enveloped,
I returned, a message in a bottle
and faded
into the expanse.

Jellyfish

My mass of cells propels
its dream, drifts on unconscious
ripples and primordial vibrations,
yields to cooler saline currents,
flinches from sharper, harder bodies,
or invasive snatch of talons.
I respond from this hollow bell
of jelly, flicker signals of luminescence
across my own transparency,
my gossamer vulnerability.
Though I stream my bane of tentacles of Medusa hair
behind me, I do not spare the unguarded;
more alien than human,
unworldly, I exist.

Distance Of The Moon

Your face warps in this distortion
of atmosphere, our memory freezes here.
Communication garbles and words blur
from the depths of these craters.
I have lost all connection to any base,
all ability to relate, umbilical, has been cut loose.
Perhaps I heard flickers of your voice
at first; a lodestar to call me home,
though I have travelled too far now
to turn back.
My feet, still heavy in even the lightness
of lunar gravity, are flightless
across these basalt plains -
to reach this Sea of Crises,
to flag the soil of Stygian mariners.

And succumb to grief –
for I did not want to find the shine
of this rock to be no more than
the reflection of some faraway star.

And anguish, anger even –
that there is this unbreachable space between us;
to have nothing left more than earthly memories,
when I have seen so many unspoken abuses
and you, I've viewed now,
from the distance of this moon.

Lately

Lately, the past has slipped
its oily fingers into my present.
A vampire, it does not nourish,
though it compels submission
and I have succumbed to its bites,
its glides, the incessant drub
of silence with its owlish wings.
The search is relentless,
to tear and punish what it finds,
while shielded from the eyes of day.
This night time raptor never sings,
in the hush to swoop and clutch
at the midnight offerings
of my unquiet mind.
I do not tell you about my undead past,
or my worry for what each sunrise brings.
We do not talk about the torments
of these internal haemorrhages.

II
I Dream In Portents
That I Am Winter In Full Bloom

Thoughts Of Revenge

No man tells you
his name is Truth with irreverence,
followed by what seems a tall tale,
but he said that Artio, a minor goddess,
had belched him out,
no more than a hiccup, in fact
and seen so, was dismissed
with the cruelty of a godly clout.

Strike one for divinity.

Nevertheless, the act of this emission,
this phlegm, entailed a clamour
of growls, as if an engine had started –
more than a cough or a cleared throat,
it was the scorch of motor,
an ejection of truth
to make way for the lie.

Up she had vented, discoloured,
sulphuric, a mottle of moulder
crept beneath her skin.
It would have been better
to have borne this restless creature,
if only her belly could have tolerated
the mortal hairball of him.

Truth said that revenge was inevitable;
it rose, a boil of plotted thoughts
of how he would strike back for man.

These overwrought thoughts drew the magpies,
who chattered him to a threshold of insanity
and mawkish at this feast,
they flew too close to his brain.
He read their entrails which, inspected,
reflected the irony of his own turmoil –
it is hard to ignore such omens,
even in the face of obvious obstacles:
how can you defeat this pantheon
when they are neither really dead or alive?

But, he declared, you could mount
a relentless assault to wear them down –
an accumulation of acts to inflict humility
and sorrow. To swat them
from the heavens as you would
the irritation of a persistent fly.
You could inspire regret over time,
he said.

When we observed a dead fox
in the road, the disharmony
of wild against tarmac,
we appraised the corpse:
dressed as Autumn,
woolly tailed, canine,
ignominious in death.
Its mouth kinked lop-sided,
as if a snarl had been a final gesture
and whilst useless now, this yellowed fang
gave emphasis to the dishevelment
that mortality brings -
nothing escapes this last indignity,
once it's kicked the bucket.
Truth announced that this was an example
of how he had struck back
against his own inglorious beginnings –
to repress what wildness nature had created,
with the slow grind of the body mechanic.

Did this count as revenge? This impotent fang.

Who knows if this is what he had planned –
this breed of concrete, the spurious seep and rise,
bleak and furious, when we are all, in a sense, damned
in the same breath.
And as if this consciousness glided across a membrane
of his mind, he made an attempt to conceal his blunder,
even from himself.
Let us apportion the blame without fairness,
let us manipulate and conceal,
let's move on and not dwell

on this swell tide of truth;
we will find there is little poetry to be discovered in dishonesty
and whilst his progenitor rolls in rage and thunder,
she sends new plagues
and we all suffer the hubris.

Ice Age

Here, at night, a bird-less wind sings its warnings;
unhindered and still, the searchlight moon
discovers you on this draped wedding gown of snow.
My feelings are preserved in permafrost
for all the other men defeated on approach,
pierced as they were by this cold that bores you hollow.
This horizon-less ice age, this glaciation,
suspends you frozen and lost on treeless tundra,
without map or reference.
What Arctic hare or fox know
of the hot spray of blood - the brutishness
that reckons success or failure
in each moment – the jag of it,
before you too join the bodies buried
amongst the ribbons and lace,
beneath the whiteness, under the silence.

Do Come In

Mind your step on the carcasses
and please don't dawdle by these stiff remains,
I must draw out the hemlock
before I knit confessions
with the bones.
Yes, it's hard to keep the place tidy;
the deaths of ortolans,
their little skeletons crunched behind napkins,
these small corpses
are daily prevalent in my mind.
And as this ice melts, I can't help but count the bodies
that surface, thawed to resurrection.
Do sit down, yes, there's room,
if you all move up a bit.
Please pay no attention to all the lovers
I have welcomed between my hospitable thighs;
most did not deserve the reception
and now just add to the clutter.

To tell you the truth, to be serious
for a moment – this is how I bared myself –
the twist of hair that unfurled and fell
across the white of my back,
reflected in a mirror, which without judgement,
showed me the stark and hot emptiness of the act.
No need to undress from names,
when it is simpler to unveil only my skin;
this kind of nakedness is an intimacy, isn't it,
that, at least, conceals the soul?

I have kept warm on the coal of these thoughts.
I fire the furnace to throw on any soft-boiled words,
watery enough to raise a feeble hiss.
I cast in any promises pledged, too –
none bright enough to light the dark.
These are all the ephemera
I reach for, but never quite grasp.
These twigs I rub together,
in the hope of some eventual spark.
Love that I thought could be earned
was never repaid or returned.

I craved and yearned and pleaded for it.
Any affection has been no more than a loan.
And thank you, your offer of religion is kind,
but, as you can see here now,
I have one of my own.

Where I Belong

When I first breached the sea,
my gills gasped their dissonance,
desperate in the air.

My tail flailed for survival,
no part of me fit for
where I found myself,
scales aflame, cast
on the saw teeth of sand,
this unforgiving universe
of sky and bird and land.

A body that once moved fluid,
now senseless and
ever more motionless.

Sun overcame
my unwatered flesh,
eyes unshined,
life dimmed,
in this fish far from home,
for I am not where I belong.

Bad Penny

In a one am lull, the wind drops
to a hesitation of held breath.
It stops the mechanic of clocks that chime
and drum up the business of time,
as an incubus finds its way in, fluid,
through a keyhole
and innocence retreats.

These visions I have, with the glass eyes of a mare,
of chest riders in bad penny dreams,
that wend their way into my slumber,
as if they were troops who march in step with my heartbeat,
or psychic utterances made wild-eyed and prostrate,
or shadows that pool in frailer folds of the mind,
as we peer in and scry for our own reflection,
but find only skewed, distorted words splayed out
like inky webs on blotting paper –
words that rise up in a sudden panicked flutter
of wings that dart for refuge back to their alphabet.

Incantations dissolve to whispers, as the tall pines and spruce
in the forest bugle to the sky and clouds charge across it
on horseback, the hounds of hours
restrained on leashes - and I wake from my dreams,
uncertain and afraid, to find myself in a hunt for dawn.

Though I don't believe in these symbols or magic anymore,
do I? The gods, the tea leaves and entrails,
or fate, or the taboo of words,
the auguries of all these ever present birds,
or the power of dreams, no –
I do not think I can live under the sway of such things.

You Became A Thorn

When the sky surrenders, distended
with weather, tangled and interned,
it ushers a new reality: dark confetti
is thrown into the moment
of startled starlings, who soar
and stir these leaves to fall
from our heavy branches.
And you begin to be a moon
that reaches its tentacles of smoke-light
to make a shadow of my elder.
You are a march of bitter bites of ants
and with bee-sting words
and nettle promises,
you become a thorn.

Nightingales

These plain nightingales are monks
who chant in secret,
hymns of constellations,
cloistered in brown robes, to hide
and stalk the refectories
of their woodland floors,
blended to this umbered domain.
All the brightness is in the notes
that ring out; we could hear
the magic of it,
as if the sepia of their plumage
had drawn the colour out
and thrown it into the air
as new quavers that voice
our more modest hopes and wishes.
They sing their nocturnal prayers
for spring and love,
a dance of fantails
and nests of dark emeralds.

Poems To The Dead

I knew the square around the chin
when I saw him again,
recognised the genetic material
that I have seen in the mirror;
a shuffled pack of cards.

And time had dulled the serrated
edges of his hands and removed his spleen
but, underneath the weakening creep
of age, the manipulation still lingered
in his later diluted words.

Wingless crows and I plough
this narrow furrow of numbness, seekers
of sanctuary, though with abraded thoughts
and emotions that were stunted years ago,
when I remedied them as warts.

These are my black blooms,
my song-less hymns;
this is my own bed of loam,
my sermons of unforgiveness,
for creatures that can't fly home.

These are the bars to my cell,
so bury him deep with feet of lead
and tie him fast there, please,
whilst I bear witness to the perversity
of poems written to the dead.

A Year And A Half On Saturn

On Saturn, I am little more than a baby.
I can walk and point,
I can falter my first few words.
I am a moonlet trapped to spin
a narrow furrow within these rings,
a ballerina of ice, who pirouettes
my solitary planetary orbit.
And when I sleep, I dream
in mustard clouds and metal storms
that whisper of how I am confined
to this cyclical repetition of ellipses -
the same place over and over,
around and around again –
to a crescendo of panic and frustration.

What I long for is the solace
of a hint of acceptance,
before I crash
and run aground upon this mass
that, I think, pretends to be a sun,
in its pallid fade of yellow,
this land of dead canary.
And these urges and desires I have,
despite the knowledge
that, underneath these atmospheric whorls
where it rains diamonds,
a year and a half will be counted
as half a lifetime of regret.

Victorian Egg Collectors

Great Auk eggs rest in nests
of tissue in tidy boxes,
darkened in drawers,
their marbled, hollow shells
sheltered from daylight's weapons
that might shatter and fade,
that might invade this motherless
incubation of sterility.

I have wept ink pools of tears
for my mother,
cried her name at night,
tried to muffle its utterance
with a closed fist pressed
to my mouth, as my brain
shrieked of its incongruence,
here in adulthood.

Who hid them in these shaded
jewellers' cabinets, their brittle cases
pin-holed and lives siphoned out?
What empty men stole them
from their hapless mothers?
I imagine these men give hard,
dank pinches of kisses,
lips tight and pursed to perfunction,
rigid jaws cranked to expose
they are, themselves, grave-robbed coffins.

I have been easy prey to,
maternally abandoned to,
these barbed wire men.
I have been in the clutches
of too many of these Victorian
egg collectors, who cold-grip you,
who are rain at night that torrent
their cool onyx drops to overwhelm
the banks of my black river, as it floods.

III

Questions That Are Clenched Fists,
But The Answers Are Just Stones

Repatriation To Self

Slender birches stand guard;
their dark eyes watch
from bone-washed bark
at the yawn of my cave,
its stones are teeth
that pack a mouth that talks
in sacred casted lots of Yew.
It has always been hard for any god
to make an inroad here,
each advancement takes you
blacker and deeper.
I am a canary in this coal mine,
a caged sentinel,
but I begin to feel
a breeze that eases
the hotter stings of violence.
The cooler repatriation to self
must purge this Ankou from me,
or he will pluck my yellow feathers,
scoop out my soul
and slurp at it as soup.
He will eat my poetry.

'The Fish Cannot Love The Fisherman' *

You may dangle bait that glints
a startle of shimmer, or flakes
the lure of morsels,
fragments of debris
that break and sink
to my depths,
a fall of snow against a blacker canvas,
but I will not surface for bird crumbs or, witless,
take in hook again, barb to cheek.
And I cannot offer the forgiveness
that I, fish-brain, suspect
you almost seek.
I hear how the waves sigh,
when they meet the sough of the wind.
I have felt the fracture force
of your abuse, eye
to splintered eye and prey that I am,
I swim deeper, I plunge.
We should be oceans apart
and now I know the anguish
of that obscured snare, no fish
could ever be prevailed upon
to love the fisherman.

*Girolamo Dandini (in Latin) Hieronymus Dandinus (1554–1634)

Therapy

My parts are constructed
to be functional.
I am blue sky. Cloudless.
I can be suppressed into a uniform
and know the right words
to express all the surfaces
of what I suffer
and dismiss,
dismiss,
there is no meaning to this,
to me or this.
Elastic, I can stretch, or be pulled.
I can be enthusiastic
in public. I can joke, I can smile
and yes, life can be painful,
with a capital P, of course,
but at a distance,
a distance away from me.

I can laugh, groan, look surprised, Oh!
in mostly the right places,
perhaps just off cue, here and there
and I don't meet your gaze,
but can raise my eyes enough
to be passably human.
It is impossible not to feel so alone,
but the sinew and gristle
is well covered with skin,
there is no way in, to know me,
my torn muscle and fractured bone.

But this insistence on feeling upon feeling,
where the colder mortuary slab of thought
was king, until I am dark clouds
and fury, black-eyed, storm-faced.
Then, rain and such sorrow,
sorrow that shakes the warblers
from their branches.
And past the self-pity and confusion,
past the history
and all the missed chances

and past so much regret and fear,
is a rebirth of me
and a very new and
very private liberty.

Confessional

I lie here, hands clasped
across bosom, in imagined scene
of my deathbed. I see
this host of hawkish pickpockets
have crannied their way back in.
And these thoughts,
these dogs that bark.
I think, as I shift my much alive hands,
that death would, at least,
free me from them.

I remember your hands.
Soft. Warm.
They could be.

Yesterday, I walked home
to another man.
I saw a feather in levitation,
but could not spot its owner,
hidden or departed, fleeting
as a thought of you.

I wonder if you know
that you do not love me,
only my memory alone.

Or, less than that – you love
a fantasy version of me
that you concocted.

And I do not know why
I have done half the things
I have, so why should you?
Though, if you choose to kneel
and confess your reasons,
I'll hear them.
But, when we are all creatures
of creation and destruction,
it could not bring the relief I seek.
If it is true that I am not dead,
then there still remains

something that is rotten
and if these poems are a confessional,
then you must be my priest.

Weather Warning

Last week, it began to rain
from my fingertips
and triggered flood warnings
in the West.
Yesterday, lightning
escaped from my ears
and caused a mystery
of thunder-snow and a biblical hail
of lost larks
to be reported
on the six o'clock news.
I see that I am not dead,
after all
and these new senses awaken
to overthrow my past suppression.
And today, in the midst
of this expression,
I opened my mouth to speak
and the sun fell from the sky;
this embered stone dropped,
as if it had slipped and
lost its bearings.
We live now in this night
of dark weather.

Bring My Slippers

We must participate with willing faces;
conventions prevail, even at bleary eyes
of seven o'clock, pinstriped at station,
where we assemble our own importance, implore
black blur of coffee to quell the nausea.
We formulate our exteriors, let them unfold
as clean sheets, ready for nine,
when we will prop ourselves up on long check lists,
to last until five – to tick and earn our worth.

But inside, as the day ripens,
I swing a loaded gun of hours around,
to watch arseholes duck as they come within my firing range.
By the afternoon, I cross a gorge
on a wood-wormed bridge and wonder
whether to push everyone else off,
to ensure that I, at least,
make it to the other side.

I nod, yes, yes,
I behave with sobriety and sugar my smile,
I make polite conversation
so that, as evening arrives,
when my camel's hump is empty
and I am hunched on gnarled knees in a desert,
I invite the ravens to pick off
all these pests I seem to have accumulated.
And I beg the questions of the day:
Did you emulate? Have you reached an impasse?
Do the doors swing open and let you in?

But then, I am in a saloon,
I sing thigh-slapping Dixie tunes,
I am Scarlett O'Hara at ten o'clock
and drink in hand, I will tolerate,
I will tolerate, head cleaved in two,
because what one thinks,
what one says,
what one delivers to the day,
is not what was considered
at midnight, with my shotgun,
before slippers and bed.

Neptune's Children

Your blues are indigo and
reeled around by unlucky moons.
Existence has marked us;
you lapsed into a fury
that spun you helpless
for so many years —
but your surface ocean of calm conceals
the lusts and troubles,
the dark spot that swirls
and bubbles beneath your exterior.

Were you closer to the sun once?
Her hot breath on your skin,
or was it mine?

I wonder what hides in these unseen reaches,
if you have gentler waves and
dunes that shimmer
and seashells on your beaches.
I wonder if dolphins cavort their joy
in your waters and if these moons
and stars will inspire revolutions at your borders.

All those hopes I allowed myself,
my fruitless, wasted, misplaced wishes.
I wanted my skies to be charged
with a surge of ascension in flights of wings,
I wanted my seas to be coursed by
the darts and flashes of silvered fins,
I wanted a religion of our love.

Of course, I tried to force your hand,
but I could not grasp or hold onto you —
we both clutched at only
the insubstantial gases from which we were made.
But I am finished now
with my patricidal wars,
have raised these flags of peace
or surrender.
And we cannot halt all the tides,
or shelter from every rain,

we cannot reverse time,
though it seems possible to draw us back in mind,
we may never be able to excommunicate the past,
but perhaps we will each find new gods.

Venus In Bed

I wear satin pyjamas
and am slippery on the sheets.
I prop myself up on novels
and thumb through pages of Austen.
Their paper flesh rasps
in my bored hands,
as I sigh with disillusionment
into a pillow.
I savour braver words
with my tongue, but stifle
the choke of sweeter, sugary ones,
as I draw the duvet up higher,
around the Regency porcelain of my neck.
I have retired from pursuits
of those haughty, slick-loined heroes,
but perhaps this is what has invited
the ennui to my bedside.
I stretch out languid thighs,
let the book drop,
welcome imagination
of deleted, steamier scenes
and wait for dawn and its chorus
to turn back the pages of the night.

Jay

I walk into the forest;
its enclosure is parental,
something almost unrecognisable to me.
An escape from the deserts of psychopaths,
who don't bring their razors
and blood spatter here.
I flit and dart the ivy,
beside the embryos of mistletoe.
Under these green beams
and shade, I am a jay.
I gather and gather,
I show the oak the blue girdle
of my dolour and unmuted,
the surprise of my voice
is an alarm call,
even to myself.
I talk to the acorns,
these glossy nuts that I will bury
to examine later.
The moss roams and spreads
its fleshy upholstery of secrets
of a soft wildness and in this viridescent array,
do you hear me?
I am noisier now, harsher in expression,
though still taking refuge in my hiding places,
I retain the reticence of a jay.

Not Yet, Not Yet

I envy the goldfinches,
the tremor of their voices
from fruiting branches, coloured
tail to beak to crimson faces
which, as if dipped in blood,
reveal hidden transgressions.

What small sins they must be
to blush their little features,
or I wonder if an innocent
curiosity allowed a cruelty to enter:
an Old Testament trespass.

And my limp words wrestle
to unlayer my misdeeds,
but there has been more or less
choice in parts, more or less
understanding at times,
more or less crimes,
though which was my original sin?

I have let these terrors in,
though I am afraid of monsters,
but also that the monster
could, in fact, be me;
that if I look down, I will see
that the claws and fangs are mine.
I am afraid of death, perhaps,
or is the real terror that I am not?
Or do I fear the restless
offspring delivered of boredom?

These are the questions that I allow
to quell, though unsettled
and I have quieter storms now.
There is the blithe music of gore-faced
finches and a promise of peace
in this psithurism of apple trees;
no night of punishment takes me,
not yet, not yet.

IV

In This Story, The Heroine Dies, Then Learns To Live Again

Release

There was no wisdom in misanthropy -
it hadn't suited me.
With thoughts arranged in their cold cages,
feelings numb as ancient insects in amber,
I disappeared, salt dissolved in water –
transparent and undefinable even to myself.
This was a repression that led to nullification:
a curtain that fell, gradual enough
to be imperceptible, or a magician's trick;
I was there and then I was not.

Oh, it exerts a deep breath to exist in a moment,
a relief, at first, valves released,
but now I think you always find yourself
in search of a destination.
No thirst is quenched in a life narrowed
to little more than dry functions, is it?

I want to wish again,
but not those rueful ones – those wishes
where I grieve for a knowledge not possessed
before the acts or events.
I wish I had known, I'd say,
I wish I had known.

Or those granite beliefs
that had insisted upon themselves
for so long, those mute, carved idols
that I had knelt before - my piety -
at which I have wailed, unheard,
for the things I have done,
for the things I have not done.
The old mothers, the shame of the men
and all the others I might rejoin.

The men I have tried to appease,
some who I might revisit... please, I urge myself, no!
At least I am finished with war,
at least that much is true.
And I have a new face that looks less alien,
has a less Uranian pallor;

it glances back at me
with curiosity in the mirror.
And perhaps, despite my battle's excarnation,
my body has reabsorbed a soul,
a robin for this winter.
When I return, I am more whole,
poetry is more of a companion or
a shy nakedness.
I send this to myself: a love letter.

What If We Are On Our Own?

Faded stars are welcome here,
wounded planets,
cratered moons.
Bring your canyons of ice
and angry peaks,
show me the hidden oceans
of your shame.
Bring your damage
and dark matter -
we will mend these broken things.
Because I wonder,
what if this is all there is,
what if you and I are the same bird
that once united, sings
and what if we are alone
in the universe?

New World

I have traced this route with astrolabe
and compass, followed the suggested paths
of constellations and under sextant
set to North Star, I smoothed out the paper of maps
stained by wind and sea, brined hair lashed
to my wide-eyed face from heavier storms,
as I sight new land on the horizon.
That first rush of fear and jubilation sobers:
the twist and yank of stomach -
should I turn back?
Perhaps these shores weren't meant for me.
I, who have fought an octopus
and lost, outnumbered by eight arms
and its slippery alienation.
I, who have shot down the albatross,
who stole shivers of fishes from my nets.
I, who cut my own anchor loose,
throwing caution to self-destruction.
To acclimatise to this new weather,
I take baby steps.
I am dazzled by the shimmer of greens
and blues in their shifted shades;
the unusual dress and practices of the natives,
who speak and move in love and safety.
Their stars are closer,
their waters are calm and free.
My stilted language, my strange words;
I do not know if they will be able to understand me.

Light

I can name these silences,
with my tongue restored.
The stories I had told myself were untenable,
under this interrogation lamp,
became mountains of truth that buckled skyward
and stretched to the horizon.

From where and how I started -
as a fledgling blinded by the weather
and a preoccupation with the traps
of others I must avoid -
with this reality of rocks and boulders
in my sight now,
I see that we are as much united
as parted by our regrets and sorrows.

We throw our stones into the water,
we spin, small as we are,
bend time together,
share dust and atoms,
particles that glitter
in waves of refracted light.
We imagine and create:
love both exists
and resists – it rests between us.

Pretty Boy

Yesterday:

I sat upon my perch,
I scratched,
I hung from the swing,
blunted my beak.
At the midday peak of my confinement,
I gazed between the bars at the clock
that hangs resigned from wall.
The clock that watches while I watch it back.
The back that needs to be watched,
the watch that needs to be clocked.
I regard time in all its divisions,
nod and bow to the elapse of
minutes and hours.

I shriek in the tongues I have learnt.
I can squawk out lines of Sophocles
and swear in French and Portuguese –
these small efforts seem to please
my happy keeper.
Lost in these alternate configurations,
I pull and tug at my harlequin feathers.

Today:

I pretend to be a chameleon,
to dissemble and disguise in ripples of coloured shifts.
I and my swivelling eye, we sigh from my branch of discomfort,
to consider if there is something to be revealed in a lunatic's hair -
look at all these modern mad dictators!
Or something unnatural and cartoonish, anyway.
A means of identification.
For a moment, I think I must be a fucking genius,
but then I wonder if this is something I have heard before,
from someone and somewhere else. It often is.

Their hair mesmerises though, doesn't it?
I imagine my keeper's hand, lost
in a maze of thatch, as one of them tells her
about affairs of state – her hand would come out,

less one finger, at least.
She'd say, darling, you fight a dirty war
and he'd say, yes, but isn't dirty nice?
as he pulled her innards from his sleeve,
like a crimson stream of handkerchiefs.

Tomorrow:

I'll be more philosophical, perhaps –
because there must be some empathy,
beneath the guffaws and bellows.
Underneath the dark ascent of smog
of this post-modern fascism, something humane
must underlie the baboonery; a bright bird.
Something that connects us all, electrical,
when we stop pretending to be who we'd prefer,
when we're not trying to be real,
when we're not playing out the irony
and cliché of every fucking neurosis,
beyond the working and earning and spending,
the genuflecting, the yessing, the seeming unending
extension of our hearts to yet more vacuity.

I watch the six o'clock news with her,
see how they lay the broken remains out after a crash,
as if they plan to rebuild the plane.
I have tried to set my past out too,
in its component parts, to fathom some logic
to my arrival in this place, here and now.
I suppose you may as well ask a river why
it bends blue or grey, this way or that.

I say, who's a pretty boy then? Pretty boy. Pretty boy.

The day after:

They will bring the bodies home in bags,
they will lay them down in neat lines,
a queue of dead.
Despite all this, children will laugh again,
people will dance in the dirt of it,

kick up their heels and smile.
There will be trembles of first kisses
and even more meaningless encounters.
More stars will tumble from their glittered settings
in a radioactive rage. Despite everything.

And I will continue with these facile performances.
I will attempt to reconcile my prismatic majesty
to the stainless steel of this cage.

They will say this was a golden age.
It always was.
And they say history repeats and perhaps it does,
again and again,
because, when we abandon the drama and artifice,
I think there has only ever been
this same soft simple concoction
of love and pain.

Crown Of Eggshell

In the myth of me, I am geese
in flight, in reverse.
And I dream in portents,
that I am winter in full bloom.
Ballads of me are discordant;
they are whale song under a moon,
full at noon. There are tales of me,
where I am the hanged man,
strung upside down.
I have questions
that are clenched fists,
but the answers are just stones.
I forget my own name
in this saga of mine.
In this story, the heroine dies,
then learns to live again,
with love and pain.
Told end to start, she exists
in twilight, crown of eggshell,
magnificent and mundane.

Sparrows

I see how the light falls,
to project this shadow,
that magnifies the objects
in its wake.
Some of these – silhouettes
of past deeds - gather
in twilight, dressed
as sparrows on a wire.
And I tell you: look up –
watch how I turn
the stars to rocks.
Yet, they continue to gutter
in distant nebulae,
their brightness still escapes and
elastic, stretches to retinas.
Diffused across my outer reaches,
they reveal a latent trail to home.

You Are The Miracle

You use ordinary words to say the extraordinary,
you weave them, coloured strands that brighten
and fall as blossom and then bruise
on the incongruity of uneven paving.
You conduct your thoughts
as music on the air
and given this voice,
it removes all choice but to listen. Listen –
I know that you do not know
what you can accomplish or endure,
until you are doing it.

As you marshal these mysteries,
you seem in communion with the dead.
The glass moves in jerks
beneath your bloodless fingers,
to letter-spell hidden messages,
that reveal only your inner dialogue.
I turn up the lamps
on these séances; I want to invite the light
back in and banish the vultures
of these shadows.

You want to force your resistant hands
together, in a long forgotten prayer
to a god in whom you no longer believe,
penitent palms pressed
to each other, when no wonder
is worthy of any clasped handed
entreaty to the ether,
when you are the miracle.

Song Thrush

Her black eye shines
its obsidian mirror;
her beak, a tiny dirk.
I thought I saw a glimmer
of consciousness ruffle
the feathers that truss
her avian strife.
What message is sent,
from eye to birdbrain,
when she spies on me or you?
Where do we fit into
her considerations
of the sky and worms?
We see there is a freedom
to live outside the cage,
but what if we have just lost sight of
the bars that confine us?
Because that bell in the distance
swings, even if we don't hear it toll.
A consolation to know then, isn't it,
that this trilling bird
contains a little heart
that staccatos the tango
of her magnificent soul.

A Homecoming

I notice the orbs of dew
that glow along the blackthorn stems,
with their deep amethyst fruits -
little lights that glister -
and am patient in anticipation of their fall
from my morning spot
at kitchen window.
Glad, I think, that my bare feet
perched, cold on the stone,
are here to feel again.

I am heartened by the omnipresence
of the wintering sun on green faces,
but sense its impermanence too,
as we glimpse the countenance
of time as it alters, as it passes.
It is for me to pacify the inchoate
impulses and voices for each day.
We exist in the doing;
all this middle-aged Buddhist wisdom.

There is a temptation to be a migration
of swallows or swifts, lost to the compulsion
to be future, to be in tomorrow,
before it has even arrived -
and the past, that fucking beast -
but what will come first: the emptiness of forgetting
or the hollowness of being forgotten?

These gathered drops of dew will fall,
impelled by wind and gravity;
they will be graceful even in their messy splash.
I am filled with a love that is afraid,
but there is beauty to my damage
and there is dignity in the fall,
there is a grace to it all.
The sun too will founder
daily on horizons.

Come, sit by me then –
let the moon be our lighthouse,

our nightly beacon of consolation
that each day will tread a tender homecoming.
And I wonder if it was not hope,
after all, but I, alone, who had returned,
divested of those gods of dread,
before whom I had quaked.
We will wonder together.

Author's Profile

Rachel Deering lives in Bath with a man and a cat.

She is a teacher.

She loves history, nature and literature. Has been published in a few anthologies and magazines, here and there.

Further titles published by Cerasus Poetry:

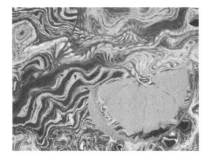

painting for lemonade
by
sj howarth

Last Night I Met John Adcock
by
Ewan Lawrie

OUTBRANCHING
by
Scharlie Meeuws

I dreamt I wrote another me
by
Alex Smith

Waiting For Another Velvet
Morning
by
Julia Macpherson

Swim With Me In Deep
Water
by
Penny Sharman

Cerasus Poetry Sampler

featuring extracts from our
first 6 titles

According To The
Dandelions
by
John Wilks

Printed in Germany
by Amazon Distribution
GmbH, Leipzig

17223164R00040